A Little Indian Cookbook

Rafi Fernandez

ILLUSTRATED BY JOHN FAZAKERLEY

Appletree Press

First published in 1992 by
The Appletree Press Ltd,
7 James Street South, Belfast BT2 8DL.
Copyright © 1992 The Appletree Press, Ltd.
Illustrations © 1992 The Appletree Press, Ltd.
Printed in the E.C. All rights reserved.

A Little Indian Cookbook

A catalogue record for this book is available
in The British Library.

ISBN: 0-86281-327-1

9 8 7 6 5 4 3 2 1

Introduction

"Namaste", which means "hello", "goodbye", or even "how are you?" denotes gentle respect. The folded hands indicate the grace and welcome to be encountered all over India. The mystery and beauty of India is 5000 years old: land peopled by a hundred races, speaking a hundred tongues. Give each its due cultural and religious influences and let the centuries roll on to provide a rich profusion of eating habits, each a little different, each just a little more exotic that the other. The unforgettable aroma of India is not just the heavy scent of jasmine and roses. It is also the fragrance of the spices that are so important to Indian cooking. Although the word "curry" is an English derivative of *kari* (which means spice sauce), today, with Indians widely spread in western countries, some good commercial curry powders and pastes are available on the market. These are usually blends of spices such as turmeric, cardamom, ginger, coriander, nutmeg, cinnamon and many more. Indian *Bawarchis* (master chefs), however, using their own individual spice mixes, create dishes as artists use a palette of colours. No other country can provide such a diverse spectrum of foods or promise a gastronomic adventure quite like India.

The amount of chilli, whether fresh or powder, can be adjusted. Where store-bought *masalas* (curry spice mixes) have been used, it is to simplify the recipe. These are widely available in groceries or can be obtained by mail order from various sources including my own shop, Rafi's Spice Box, 48, Gaol Lane, Sudbury, Suffolk, CO10 6JL, U.K.

The Modern Indian Kitchen

Today several commercial brands offer prepared *masalas* (blended spice mix) in powder and paste form and I find these a great boon. Test different brands to find your preference.

Varieties of *masala* mixes

Kashmiri	Mild or hot curry
Green	Madras
Garam	Pasanda
Tikka	Bhuna
Tandoori	Roghan Josh
Kebab	Vindaloo
Biryani	Dhansak

Other useful pastes

If possible, obtain the following pastes in Indian or Chinese brands as they are pure with no additives. Once opened, they will keep in the fridge for up to three weeks or they can be divided into portions and frozen.

Ginger	Garlic
Coriander	Red or green chilli
Mixed ginger, garlic and green chilli	

Other ingredients

It is also possible to obtain commercial deep-fried onion, a great time saver, with 2oz/50g equalling 1 large raw onion. Curry leaves (*Kariyapath*) and coriander leaves (*Kotmir*) are available, fresh or dried. (Fresh leaves can be washed, dried and open-frozen.)

Coconut milk (*Nariyal doodh*) is available in tins, powder form or in cream blocks. To obtain 6 fl oz/175ml thick coconut milk add 3oz/75g coconut cream to 6 fl oz/175ml boiling water. To obtain 6 fl oz/175ml thin coconut milk, add 1 oz/25g coconut cream to 6 fl oz/175ml boiling water.

Gram flour is flour made from split peas. *Gram* or *dhals* are pulses — red lentils, moong beans, and so on. The former is the whole grain seed and the latter come in split form and are sometimes washed and husked.

Khushka/Chawal

Plain Boiled Rice

Freshly-boiled rice is cooked daily all over India but favoured more in South India. Rice, the ancient sages of India believed, is a gift of the gods, and its preparation is a form of prayer.

---

12 oz/350g/1 1/2 cups Patna or Basmati rice
18 fl oz/500ml/3 cups water
1 tsp butter, vegetable or olive oil
1/2 tsp salt or to taste

Pick and wash the rice in several changes of water. Allow to soak for 30 minutes (if possible) for fluffier, cooked grains. Drain well and put the rice in a heavy pan which has a tight-fitting lid. Add the measured water, butter or oil and salt. Bring to boil, turn the heat to very low, cover and cook for 12–15 minutes. To serve, loosen the rice with a flat slotted spoon to release the steam and prevent damaging the grains.

Bhaghara Khushka (Pulao Rice)

First sauté the drained rice in butter or oil with 1/2 tsp black cumin seeds, I in piece of cinnamon stick, 2 green cardamoms and 2 bay leaves. Add the water and salt and proceed as for plain boiled rice.

When the rice is cooked, lift the lid and pour the food colour of your choice mixed in a little milk on the surface of the rice at random. Cover the pan and rest for 5 minutes before serving as above. Garnish with browned onions and almond flakes.

Naan

Leavened Bread

The variety of Indian breads is infinite but the *naan* is by far the most popular one in the western world. Although, traditionally, they are baked in a *tandoor* (clay oven), they are just as delicious baked in an ordinary oven.

I tsp sugar	I tsp salt
I tsp fresh or dried yeast	I egg yolk beaten or
5 fl oz/150ml warm water	a little milk
8oz/200g plain flour	2 tsp poppy/onion/sesame
3oz/75g melted ghee or	seeds (or mixed)
unsalted butter	

Place the sugar, yeast and warm water in a cup. Whisk well and rest until it turns frothy. Sieve the flour and salt. Make a well and pour in the yeast mixture along with the *ghee* or butter. Mix together with your fingers. Now rub your palms with a little *ghee* or butter and make a smooth and soft dough. Knead for about 5 minutes. Rest dough covered for 2 hours

or more to rise. Divide into 6 portions and gently roll out on a lightly floured surface. Brush with egg or milk and sprinkle on the seeds. Place on greased baking tray and bake for 10–15 minutes in a pre-heated oven gas mark 8, 450°F, 230°C. Serve immediately or keep warm wrapped in tinfoil.

Gosht Biryani

Rice Layered with Meat

Id-ul-Fitr marks the end of the Ramazan fast at the appearance of the new moon. *Fitr* means five pounds of grain which is distributed to the poor. *Biryani* is truly a jewel made for a royal treat and therefore a favourite with the *Noobs* of Hyderabad. Served with Egg and Tomato Curry (p. 40) and a *raitha* (p. 12), it cannot fail to please.

5 fl oz/150ml milk	1 tsp turmeric powder
1 sachet saffron powder	salt to taste and 1 tsp sugar
6 tbsp lemon juice	2 lbs/900g cubed lamb or boned
4 green chillies, finely chopped	chicken
4 oz/100g fresh coriander, chopped	1 lb/450g Basmati rice
	1 tsp black cumin seeds
5 fl oz/150ml natural yogurt, beaten	4 green cardamoms
	2 in cinnamon stick
4 tbsp biryani masala	6 tbsp melted ghee or unsalted
2 tbsp garam masala	butter

Mix the milk and saffron and keep aside. Mix the next 8 items and marinade the lamb or chicken in it for 4–6 hours. Gently cook it for 45 minutes in a heavy pan. Meanwhile, wash the rice and cook with whole spices in boiling water until the grains are a quarter done. Drain.

Grease the base of a heavy pan and place half the rice in an even but loose layer. Spread the cooked meat mixture with all the juices over the rice. Spread the remaining rice over this in a loose neat layer. Pour the saffron milk over the rice at random spots. Finally pour the *ghee* or butter over the rice. Grease a circular piece of foil (the size of the pan) and place it greased side down on the rice. Cover the pan and cook on low to medium heat for about 20 minutes or until the rice is fluffy. Gently toss the rice and meat together before serving.

Raitha

Yogurt, Mint and Cucumber Salad

---

10 fl oz/300ml natural yogurt, beaten
2 tsp mint sauce (or to taste)
salt and sugar to taste
4oz/100g cucumber, thinly sliced
1/2 tsp paprika
fresh mint leaves for garnish

Mix the first four ingredients gently together and chill. Garnish with paprika and mint leaves and serve.

Roghan Josh

Lamb in a Deep Red Sauce

A visit to Kashmir is incomplete until you have stayed on a houseboat on the beautiful Dal lake and eaten meals cooked by the *khansaba* (cook) on the kitchen boat which travels alongside the main houseboat.

I tbsp ghee *or vegetable oil*
$^1/_2$ tsp asafoetida powder
I lb/450g cubed lean lamb
5 fl oz/150ml natural yogurt
beaten with $^1/_2$ tsp cornflour
2 tbsp roghan josh
I tsp kashmiri masala
I tsp garam masala

8–10 saffron strands or
I sachet powdered saffron
$^1/_2$ tsp sugar
salt to taste
4 tbsp tomato purée
blanched almond flakes
for garnish

Heat the *ghee* or oil in a heavy pan and fry the asafoetida and lamb on a medium heat until the meat pieces are sealed. Remove from the heat and cool a little. Fold in the yogurt and return to the heat and cook until the yogurt is absorbed. Add the remaining ingredients except the garnish and cook until the meat is tender and the gravy almost dry. Garnish with the almond flakes and serve hot. If you prefer a hotter curry (*phaal*), then add 2 tsp chilli powder with the *masalas* to the above recipe and you will achieve the hottest curry available in restaurants.

Rafi's Paretal

Dry Meat Curry

This recipe is dedicated to all my pupils who love it, especially Peter who made double batches in his wok that looked like a volcano erupting. It is truly a "Rafi" invention for those who like it hot.

---

1 1/2 tsp chilli powder (or adjust to taste)
2 tbsp madras curry powder
1 tsp turmeric powder
salt to taste
3 tbsp vegetable oil
2 large onions, finely sliced
2 tsp ginger, garlic and chilli paste
8 curry leaves
1 lb/450g cubed lean lamb or beef
6 fl oz/175ml thick coconut milk (p. 7)
8oz/200g tinned chopped tomatoes

Mix the first 4 ingredients with 6 tablespoons water to a smooth paste. Heat the oil in a heavy pan and fry the onions until golden brown. Add the ginger, garlic and chilli paste, curry leaves and the spice paste and fry until the oil rises above the *masala*. Add the meat and fry until evenly sealed. Lower the heat, cover the pan and simmer for about 45 minutes. Add the coconut milk and tomatoes and mix well. Simmer gently until the meat is fully cooked. Serve hot with plain rice.

Gosht Surmahi

Lamb with Fenugreek Leaves

The Kolhapuri people's food is rich, heavy in meat and full of red Sankeshwari chillies. Their ingenuity in cooking meat in a variety of pungent gravies is legendary and, although the palaces are now empty, the food has a nostalgic royal air about it.

---

2 lb/900g spring lamb, cubed
5 green cardamoms
2 black cardamoms
2 in piece cinnamon stick
4 bay leaves
Purée:
2oz/50g fresh ginger
6 cloves garlic
2 medium-sized onions
10 fresh red chillies
14oz/400g tinned chopped tomatoes
4oz/100g kasoori methi (dried fenugreek leaves)
salt to taste

Place the first 5 ingredients in a heavy pan and cover with cold water. Bring to the boil and simmer until the water has nearly evaporated, skimming any froth if necessary. Fold in the remaining ingredients and gently cook until the lamb is fully cooked and the gravy thick, about 1 1/2 hours.

Buhari Gosht

Madras-style Meat

Being locked up in a convent in Madras with a day pass only twice a year meant that the first destination pupils went to when outside was a Buhari restaurant. The Muslim chef from Southern India prepared this delicious *gosht* and let us eat as much as we could, with unlimited boiled rice.

---

4 tbsp vegetable oil
1 large onion, finely sliced
4 each of cloves and green cardamoms
4 each of fresh green and dry red chillies, chopped
1 tsp turmeric powder
4 tbsp bhuna masala
1 lb/450g lamb chops
400g/14oz tinned chopped tomatoes
salt to taste and a pinch of sugar
fresh coriander, chopped

Heat the oil in a heavy pan and fry the onion, cloves, cardamoms and chillies until the onions are brown. Add the turmeric, *bhuna masala* and chops. Sauté until all the chops are evenly sealed. Cover the pan and simmer on a very low heat for about 10 minutes. Add the remaining ingredients, reserving a little of the coriander for garnish. Cook until the chops are fully done. Garnish and serve hot. Sprinkle a little lemon juice over the meat if you wish.

Galina Xacutti

Goan Chicken

It is difficult, with just one recipe, to lead you into the sanctum of Goan (now Panjim) cuisine. The method of eating is both a meal and a ritual. The local men start drinking *feni*, a potent cashew liquor, in the afternoon to set the pace and mood for the pungent and spicy food that follows.

6oz/150g/¹/₂ cup desiccated
  coconut
2 tsp each cumin, coriander
  and mustard seeds
4 cloves garlic and I in
  fresh ginger
4 cloves and 8 peppercorns
6 whole dry red chillies
I tsp five-spice powder
I onion, chopped
4 tbsp oil

2 onions, finely sliced
I tsp turmeric
salt to taste and a
  pinch of sugar
3 lb/I.5 kg chicken,
  skinned and jointed
9 fl oz/250ml thick
  coconut milk
4 tbsp tomato purée
I tsp freshly-grated nutmeg

Dry-roast the first 7 items in a frying pan until the onion and desiccated coconut are a deep golden brown. Grind all of these in a processor to a smooth paste and reserve. Heat the oil and fry the sliced onions until brown. Add the *masala* paste, turmeric and salt. Fry for 2–3 minutes. Add the chicken and remaining ingredients. Bring to the boil, then simmer until the chicken is cooked and the gravy is thick.

Mulligatawny

Anglo-Indian Stew

An Indian mini-Amsterdam, Cochin is a complex of islands and towns linked by bridges and ferries influenced by the past — Dutch — and the present. The original *mulla-ga-tani* changed, through the Dutch influence, with addition of meats, coconut milk and tomatoes.

---

1 pt/600ml chicken or vegetable stock
1 onion, finely chopped
8 oz/200g fresh or tinned tomatoes, chopped
1 tsp each garlic and ginger paste
2 in/2.5 cm cinnamon stick
6–8 curry leaves
1 tsp each coriander and cumin powder
1/2 tsp fenugreek powder or 8–10 fenugreek seeds
9 fl oz/250ml thick coconut milk
3 lb/1.5 kg boned chicken pieces or
2 lb/900g raw king prawns, shelled and deveined
1 onion, finely sliced and deep-fried
4 tbsp lemon juice
salt to taste
a handful of fresh coriander leaves, chopped

Place the first 10 items in a large pan and bring to the boil. Simmer for about 10 minutes. Add the chicken or prawns and simmer until they are cooked (prawns require less cooking time). Fold in the remaining ingredients and serve hot.

Murgh Char Minar

Chicken from the Four Minarets

Hyderabad, my home town, has a rich and varied three-hundred-year-old history during which the Mughlai and Andhra menus have jostled side by side in unparalleled exotica. This merging of cultures is unmatched anywhere else in India.

---

1 tbsp vegetable oil
8oz/200g onion, finely chopped
2oz/50g each fresh chopped ginger and garlic paste
8oz/200g lean lamb or beef mince
1 tbsp green masala
7 fl oz/200ml natural set yogurt
4 hard-boiled eggs, coarsely chopped
4oz/100g blanched flaked almonds
2 tsp salt
3 lb/1.3 kg oven-ready chicken
1 sachet powdered saffron

Heat the oil on medium heat and fry the onions, ginger and garlic until the onions are translucent. Add the mince, green *masala* and half the yogurt and mix well. Cook until the mince is half done. Remove from the heat. Fold in the chopped eggs, half the flaked almond and 1 tsp salt. Stuff this mixture inside the chicken and tie or skewer the openings. Mix the remaining yogurt with the saffron and spread over the outside of the chicken. Sprinkle with the remaining salt. Roast in a pre-heated oven at gas mark 3, 350°F, 180°C, allowing 15–20 minutes per pound. Rest chicken for 5 minutes before carving. Serve hot garnished with the remaining almonds and a crisp green salad.

Murgh Tikka Masala

Chicken Kebabs with Sauce

The cuisine of the Punjab is known for being rich in protein and fats — both of which are necessary to keep the Punjabi temperament going at full steam. Punjabi cooking has been to concoct mouthwatering dishes many of which have reached the west, gaining immediate popularity.

---

4 tbsp tikka masala
4 oz/125g natural yogurt
salt to taste
1 tsp sugar
4 chicken breasts, skinned, boned and cubed
Sauce:
2 tbsp tikka masala
4 oz/125g natural yogurt
3 fl oz/75ml double cream
1 tsp sugar
juices collected in grill tray

Mix the first 4 ingredients and marinade the chicken for 1 hour, or longer if possible. Grill under medium heat, resting chicken on a mesh grid or on skewers. Baste and turn the chicken pieces over and grill until well-cooked with burnt spots. Keep hot. To make the sauce, mix all the ingredients in a small pan. Gently heat, stirring constantly to avoid curdling. When the sauce is smooth, the oil will float. Adjust seasoning if necessary. Pour over chicken and serve with rice or *naan* (p. 8) and a green salad.

Murgh ka Salan

Bhori-style Chicken

Festive Muslim *bhori* dinners are served on the floor on a *dastar khan* — a white linen cloth which has been delicately decorated with raw grains, flower petals and greenery. When the meal is over, all of the decorations are thrown into a river, lake or well.

---

4 tbsp vegetable oil	3 lb/1.5 kg chicken (remove
2 medium onions, finely sliced	skin and bone if you wish)
1 tsp garam masala	2 tbsp tomato purée
4 tsp bhuna masala	9 fl oz/275g tinned tomatoes
1 tsp turmeric powder	6 fl oz/175ml thick
5 fl oz/150ml water	coconut milk (p. 7)
	salt to taste

Heat the oil and fry the onions until golden brown. In the meantime mix the *masalas* and turmeric with the water. When the onions are brown add the *masalas* and fry for 3–5 minutes. Add the chicken and fry until evenly coloured. Add the remaining ingredients, mix well, lower the heat and cook covered until the chicken is done. Serve hot. (Fold in $^1/_2$ tsp sugar if you wish before serving.)

Dhansak

Hot, Sweet and Sour Potpourri

Parsis came to India from Persia bringing their own culinary genius. A reporter found a young student who read the newspaper marriage columns and thereby attended 150 Parsi feasts during his 3 years at university in Bombay.

2oz/50g each red gram (tuwar), Bengal gram (channa)
green gram (moong) and red lentils (masoor)
4 fresh mint leaves or ¹/₂ tsp mint sauce
12 fl oz/350ml water
1 large aubergine, potato and carrot
4oz/100g deep-fried onions
1 oz/25g dried fenugreek leaves
4 tbsp vegetable oil
3 tsp each of ginger, garlic, green chilli paste
3 tbsp dhansak masala
4oz/100g fresh coriander, chopped
1 lb/450g chicken portions or raw king prawns
4 tbsp lemon juice
salt to taste and 1 tsp sugar

Place the first 6 items in a heavy pan and bring to the boil. Simmer until the lentils and vegetables are soft and can be mashed with a wooden spoon. Reserve. In a separate pan heat the oil and fry the spices and *masala*, coriander and chicken pieces. When the chicken pieces are sealed add the lentil and vegetable sauce and simmer until the chicken is cooked. Add the lemon juice and seasoning and serve hot with *Baghara Khushka* (p. 8). If you use prawns, reduce the cooking time.

Porcheri

South Indian Vegetable Stew

Udipi, Vihar and Bhavan are generic names for South Indian vegetarian restaurants where food is served on banana leaves. As you unfold the banana leaf and get ready to eat, remember to sprinkle your leaf with water from the glass already set out. The waiter will not serve you until this cleansing ritual has been completed.

8oz/200g Bengal gram (channa dhal)
400g/1 lb cut mixed vegetables of your choice
1½ tsp chilli powder
1 tsp turmeric powder
salt to taste
2 tsp soft brown sugar
8oz/200g desiccated coconut
4 tbsp coconut or vegetable oil
1 tsp each mustard and cumin seeds
6–8 curry leaves

Cook the *dhal* with plenty of water until soft. Drain and reserve the water. Gently mash the *dhal* with a wooden spoon and keep aside. Cook the vegetables in the reserved water with chilli and turmeric powder, salt, sugar and half the coconut. When the vegetables are done add the *dhal* and gently fold together. Heat the oil and fry the seeds, curry leaves and remaining coconut until the coconut is light brown. Pour all this over the vegetable and *dhal* and mix well. Reheat the whole mixture and serve hot.

Gucci Mattar Paneer

Mushroom, Peas and Cheese Curry

In Rajasthan *Teej Mala* (Festival of Devi) is essentially for women and in particular mothers and their daughters-in-law. Devi, the wife of Lard Shiva, is worshipped for two days to obtain her gratitude and to give her adoration. Only vegetarian dishes are cooked by the daughters-in-law to remain in the grace and favour of the mothers-in-law. Feta can be used as a substitute for *paneer*.

Purée:	4 tbsp ghee *or vegetable oil*
8oz/200g tinned tomatoes	*1 tsp nigella seeds* (ajwain)
1 tsp each ginger and	*8oz/200g button*
garlic paste	*mushrooms, halved*
6 green chillies	*8oz/200g garden peas*
1 tsp pasanda masala	*8oz/200g paneer, cubed and*
6 fl oz/150ml double cream	*fried until golden*
1/2 tsp cornflour	*handful of fresh coriander*
1 small onion	*leaves, chopped*

Heat the *ghee* or oil and fry the nigella seeds. Add the puréed *masala* and sauté over medium heat stirring constantly. Fold in the mushrooms, peas and *paneer*. Simmer for 15 minutes. Garnish with the coriander leaves and serve hot.

Dahi-ni-Kari

Yogurt Curry

Masters of vegetarian cooking, Gujeratis make, in an endless procession, a variety of mouth-watering dishes from the simplest lentils and vegetables.

12oz/350g natural yogurt, beaten
4 fl oz/125ml thin coconut milk
4 tbsp gram flour mixed in ¹/₂ cup water
¹/₂ tsp each turmeric and chilli powder
salt to taste and ¹/₂ tsp sugar
10oz/280g corn kernels with peppers
4 tbsp vegetable oil
4 whole dried red chillies
1 tsp cumin seeds
2 cloves garlic, crushed
6–8 curry leaves
¹/₄ tsp asafoetida

Mix the first 5 items and pass through a sieve. Add corn and peppers and on a low heat cook the mixture until the sauce is smooth and thick. Set aside. Heat the oil and fry the remaining ingredients until the garlic turns golden brown. Pour the oil and spices over the yogurt sauce and cover the pan to infuse. Gently re-heat and serve plain or compliment with *Bhajias* (p. 43). If you are adding the *Bhajias* allow them to simmer in the curry for 5 minutes before serving.

Ande aur Tamatar ka Cut

Egg and Tomato Curry

This dish originated in the Deccan and the *Dakhnis* love their food hot. Traditionally served with *Biryani* (p. II), you can add vegetables of your choice to make an even more wholesome dish.

---

1 1/2 pts tomato juice
2 oz/50g coconut cream
4 tbsp gram flour (besan) *mixed in a little water*
2 tsp kashmiri masala
1 tsp garam masala
salt to taste and 1/2 tsp sugar
2 tsp each vegetable oil and sesame oil
1 tsp cumin seeds
4 whole dried red chillies
6 curry leaves
4 cloves garlic, sliced
1/4 tsp asafoetida
4 hard-boiled eggs, halved
browned onions and fresh coriander for garnish

Mix the first 6 items in a large pan and gently heat until the coconut has dissolved. In a frying pan heat the oils and fry the remaining ingredients except the eggs and garnish. When the garlic slices are a deep golden brown, pour everything over the tomato mixture and cover to allow the spice aroma to infuse. Reheat gently, float the halved eggs on top and garnish with browned onions and coriander and serve hot.

Bhajias

Savoury Fritters

At Navratri, the festival of Nine Nights during which Durga, the warrior goddess, is worshipped, people only eat light snacks like *bhajias, samosas, pakoras,* etc. India seems to have more snacks than any other country in the world.

8oz/200g gram flour (besan *or* channa atta)
1 tsp baking powder
salt to taste
$^1/_2$ tsp each turmeric and chilli powder
$^1/_2$ tsp each onion, nigella, cumin and fennel seeds, coarsely ground
2 green chillies, finely chopped
handful of fresh coriander leaves, chopped
2 large onions, finely sliced

Sieve the first 4 items in a large mixing bowl. Add the remaining ingredients and toss. Gradually add water and, using your hand, mix the ingredients in until you have folded in all the dry flour and have a thick dropping consistency batter. Heat sufficient oil for deep-frying and, when smoking hot, drop spoonfuls of the mixture and fry until golden brown. Drain well and serve or use in *Dahi-ni-Kari* (p. 39).

Ringanano Olo

Stuffed Aubergine

Sun and sand colour the lives of the Kutch, people whose lifestyle is very much a result of their desert environment. The cuisine is innovative through necessity and vegetable dishes are available only when the supply comes in from neighbouring states.

2 large deep purple aubergines	I tsp chilli powder
4 tbsp vegetable oil	I tsp each turmeric and
I tsp each mustard and	coriander powder
cumin seeds	salt to taste
8oz/200g spring onions,	$^1/_2$ tsp sugar
finely chopped	

Wash and wipe the aubergines without trimming the tails. Using I teaspoon oil rub the aubergines all over and bake in a moderately hot oven until the skins blacken. Remove, but leave the oven on a low setting. When the aubergines are cool to handle cut in half and scoop out the white pulp. Return the cases on a greased tray to the oven. Mash the pulp coarsely and reserve. Heat the remaining oil and fry the seeds and spring onions for 2–3 minutes. Add the remaining ingredients and the mashed pulp. Mix well. Re-fill the aubergine cases with the spiced pulp and return to the oven for about 20 minutes. This can also be served as a starter garnished with lemon wedges.

Tarka Dhal

Lentils Seasoned with Hot Oil and Spices

Rice and *dhal* are the mainsprings of the working man's diet. In Varanasi, one of India's oldest cities, the god Ganesh is worshipped and special foods prepared from the new harvest for a feast. Later, clay images of him are immersed into the Ganga River and sand from the river bed is sprinkled around the grain stores for his blessing.

6oz/175g/1 cup mixed red lentils (masoor)
and red grain (tuwar)
18 fl oz/500ml/3 cups water
$1/2$ tsp turmeric powder
2 whole green chillies, stems removed
1 tsp salt
Seasoning (final fry):
4 tbsp vegetable oil
1 onion, finely sliced
2 cloves garlic, finely sliced
$1/2$ tsp each of mustard, onion and cumin seeds
6 curry leaves
2 whole dry red chillies
1 tsp lemon juice and a few fresh coriander leaves

Pick and wash the *dhals* and drain. Place the first 4 ingredients in a pan and bring to the boil. Lower the heat and simmer with the pan half covered until the *dhals* are soft and most of the water has evaporated. Add salt and mash the *dhals* with a wooden spoon, adjusting the consistency, if too thick, with boiling water. Transfer to a heatproof serving dish and keep warm. In a small frying pan heat the oil and fry the onion and garlic until golden brown. Add the seeds, curry leaves and red chillies and fry for 2–3 minutes. Pour all this over the *dhals*. Sprinkle with lemon juice and coriander leaves and serve.

Patra ni Macchi

Stuffed Fish Rolls

This is a famous Parsi dish traditionally baked in banana leaves. Like the English Sunday roast this is prepared on Sundays and served along with *Dhansak* (p. 32).

---

4 fillets of Dover, lemon sole or plaice (if your fishmonger is friendly request the white fillets)
a batch of Kotmir Pudina *chutney (p. 55)*
salt to taste
4 pieces (10 in x 10 in) special cooking cling film
wedges of lemon or lime

Wash and dry the fish fillets. Rub the flesh side generously with the chutney and sprinkle salt to taste. Roll the fillets and wrap each in a piece of the cling film tying the ends together. Drop the rolls into boiling water and cook for 10–15 minutes. Remove and when cool enough to handle remove the cling film. Serve each person a roll or cut them into slices to look like 'swiss-roll' slices. Serve with lemon or lime wedges.

Sarson Jingha

Mustard Spinach with Prawns

The sea-kissed town of Konarak in the state of Orissa is a
popular tourist resort. Oriya cuisine depends on seafood and
is liberally spiced with mustard — an influence from West
Bengal — yet the food has a delectable difference.

---

1 lb/½ kg raw king prawns, shelled and deveined
1 tsp turmeric
salt to taste
4 tsp mustard or vegetable oil
¼ tsp onion seeds (kalonji)
6–8 curry leaves
2 tsp pasanda masala
15oz/450g tinned mustard spinach (sarson)
2 large tomatoes, chopped
handful of fresh coriander leaves

Rub the prawns with the turmeric and salt and keep aside.
Heat the oil on medium heat and fry the onion seeds, curry
leaves and green *masala* for 2–3 minutes. Add the prawns and
stir-fry until they are bright orange in colour. Fold in the
mustard spinach, tomatoes and coriander leaves. Heat to
serving temperature and serve with rice or bread.

Xevttallo Molee

Salmon with Chilli-Coconut Sauce

When fresh coconut, chillies and the Manglorean mind fuse, the result is pure culinary magic! Gleaned from the traditional repertoire of this coastal region, here is a classic recipe which displays the ingenuity of yet another genre of Indian cuisine.

I tsp cumin powder
1 1/2 tsp chilli powder, or to taste
1/2 tsp turmeric powder
I tbsp wine vinegar
1 1/2 tsp slat or to taste
4–6oz/175g salmon steaks or fillets
4 tbsp vegetable oil
6 fl oz/175ml/1 3/4 cups thick coconut milk (p. 7)
Purée:
I large onion
6 green chillies
4 cloves garlic
4 in piece fresh ginger
1 1/2 tsp each cumin and coriander powder

Mix the first 5 ingredients into a paste. Coat the salmon thoroughly and marinade for 30 minutes. Heat the oil and fry the puréed ingredients for 5 minutes on medium heat. Add the coconut milk and bring the sauce to the boil. Reduce the heat and gently slip in the salmon. Cook each side in the sauce for 5–8 minutes. Arrange the salmon on a warmed plate and spoon the sauce around them and serve with lemon wedges.

Kotmir Pudina Chutney

Coriander and Mint Relish

An entire book could be written on the chutneys and pickles of India. This has always been my favourite and can be used in many different ways; an accompaniment to any curry or sandwich, or mixed with natural yogurt as a variation to *raitha* (p. 12) or fish filling.

---

2 tbsp vegetable oil
2oz/50g desiccated coconut
2 green chillies and 2 dried red chillies
1/2 tsp each mustard, cumin, fennel and onion seeds
4 curry leaves
4oz/100g fresh coriander washed and drained
4 tbsp lemon juice
2 tsp mint sauce
salt to taste and 1 tsp sugar

Heat the oil and fry the next 5 ingredients until the coconut is golden brown. Cool the mixture and place in a food processor along with the remaining ingredients. Blend until the coriander is finely chopped. Adjust seasoning and lemon juice if necessary. Serve cold.

Aamba Piyali

Mango Cups

Mango is a very sacred fruit in India. It is said that Lord Shiva brought the mango tree from heaven for his beautiful wife Parvathi whose favourite fruit it was and who had become very upset when she found that mango was not available on earth. Alfonso, Rasdhara, Malgoba and Neelam are some of the Indian mangoes available abroad from Indian grocers between April and July.

---

2 ripe mangoes
4 tsp sugar
I sachet saffron powder
4 tbsp double cream

Wash the mangoes and dry them gently. Make a cut right through to the seed around the centre of each mango. Hold each mango on both sides of the cut and twist carefully. Two halves will be like cups and the other two will have the seed sticking out. Carefully remove the seeds. Scoop out the inside flesh without damaging the skins. Mash the flesh coarsely and mix in the remaining ingredients. Refill the mango cups with this mixture, chill well and serve. This is very refreshing after a spicy meal.

Shrikhand

Yogurt and Cheese Dessert

Gokulashtmi, the birthday of the Lord Krishna, is celebrated in honour of his childhood pranks. Earthen pots containing yogurt, cream and money are suspended from a huge rope on every street corner. Groups of young boys and men climb on each other's shoulders to form a human pyramid to reach and break the pots.

---

4 fl oz/110ml/^{1}/$_2$ cup natural yogurt
8oz/225g half-fat cheese
2oz/50g full-fat cheese
2–4 oz/50–100g icing sugar
^{1}/$_2$ tsp each ground cardamom and nutmeg
8–10 strands saffron or 1 sachet of powdered saffron
almond flakes and pink rose petals to garnish

Chill a large mixing bowl in the refrigerator for 1 hour. Place the cheese and yogurt in the bowl and whisk until evenly mixed. Gradually add the sugar and keep whisking until you have a light and creamy mixture. Taste as you add the sugar. You may not wish to use all of it. Add the cardamom, nutmeg and saffron and mix again. Decorate with the almond flakes and petals, chill and serve.

Index